Little Freshie and the ALPHABET VALLEY!

Volume 1

The Little Freshie Series

Freshie loves LETTERS

Ed Brinkman

Little Freshie and the Alphabet Valley
By Ed Brinkman

From the Little Freshie Series, Volume 1
© Copyright Ed Brinkman 2021

I dedicate this book to my loving family
and especially my grandkids –
From Papa Q with love.

Thank you for believing in me and encouraging me
to better myself in writing.

Meet
Little Freshie
the dinosaur!

Freshie wants to teach little kids about

LETTERS!

Once upon a time

A little dinosaur called Freshie, decided to take a long, long walk.
He greeted his mom and set out with his friend.

Just be home before dark... and whose your friend?
His name is S...???

He passed some Flamingos and asked them what is behind the hills.
The ALPHABET VALLEY, they replied, and wondered who is Freshie's friend...

Freshie got extremely excited when he sees the bright lights in the distance.
I can't wait to see the alphabet valley
Me too!
All his animal friends are also very excited when they see Freshie going to Alphabet Valley!
And they also wondered who is Freshie's friend...

ABCDEFGHIJKLMN
OPQRSTUVWXYZ

The animals at Alphabet Valley could not believe that Freshie came all the way to learn about letters.

Welcome to the Alphabet Valley

I'm finally here!

Me too!

Freshie is very excited to learn about letters...

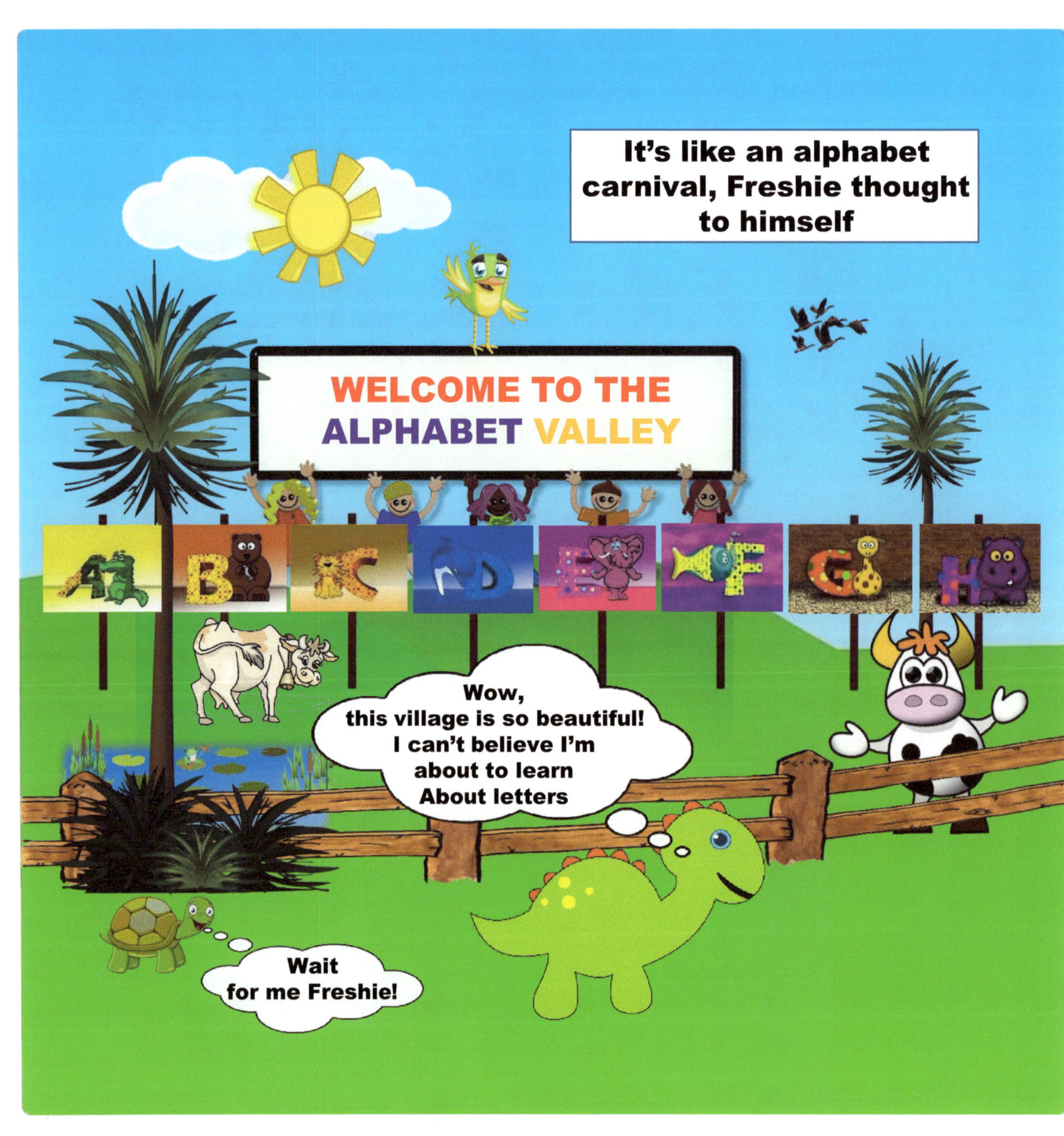

It's like an alphabet carnival, Freshie thought to himself
WELCOME TO THE ALPHABET VALLEY
A B C D E F G H
Wow, this village is so beautiful! I can't believe I'm about to learn About letters
Wait for me Freshie!

A a
Alligator

B
b
Bear

Cat

D
d
Dog

Elephant

Fish

G
g
Giraffe

Hh
Hippo

Insect

J
j
Jaguar

K
k
Kangaroo

Lion

Mm
Monkey

N
n
Nest

Owl

Pelican

Quail

R r
Robot

Squirrel

Tiger

Umbrella

Vampire bat

W
W
Whale

Xylophone

Y y
Yacht

Zebra

Freshie had such a good time at the alphabet valley that he can't wait to see what he can learn again on his next adventure.
Come Speedy! My mom said I must be home before dark.
Some of his friends came to see him and his friend off as the sun is setting. His mom did say that he must be home before dark...

Little Freshie's mom was very impressed and proud of what he has learned about letters. She was also happy to know his friend's name - Speedy.

Come let's go in, than you and Speedy can tell me all about it.
Mom you won't believe what happened today. Me and Speedy won a prize!
I made some nice chocolate wafers for you. Bring your new friend along also

Little Freshie knows now about LETTERS!

He even got a reward for knowing letters!

OH YES, his friend Speedy also knows about letters now...

Now, you do too!

Stay tuned for more
Little Freshie books